Chris Oyakhilome

LoveWorld Publications

Unless otherwise indicated, all Scripture quotations are taken from the King James Version of the Bible.

1st Edition 1997; 2nd Printing 1999

2nd Edition 1999, 4th Printing 2000

The Oil & The Mantle
ISBN 978- 34865-1- 9

Copyright ©1999 by Chris Oyakhilome

Published by LoveWorld Publications
London Address
PO Box 21520
London E10 5FG
Phone: 0181-5172367

Nigeria Address
PO Box 13563 Lagos Nigeria
Phone:01-7740243; 01-4934393
fax: 234-1-4934393

e-mail: cec@christembassy.org.
Website:www.christembassy.org.

All rights reserved under International Copyright Law.
Contents or cover may not be reproduced in whole or in part in any form without the expressed written permission of the publisher.

Table of Contents

Introduction	1
1. Being Established in Righteousness	9
2. The Oil	27
3. The Mantle	39
4. Walking By Faith	65

INTRODUCTION

Spiritual Understanding

God wants His children to have a perfect understanding of spiritual things; He does not want us to always find ourselves in a position where we don't understand what He desires of us. Talking about the day of the Church through the prophets, God said,

"For this is the covenant that I will make with the house of Israel after those days, saith the Lord; I will put my laws into their mind, and write them in their hearts: and I will be to them a God, and they shall be to me a people: And they shall not teach every man his neighbour, and every man his brother, saying, Know the Lord: for all shall know me, from the least to the greatest".

Hebrews 8:10-11

God wants us to have a personal relationship with Him through His Word.

Though He has given the five-fold ministry gifts to the Church to teach the saints, and build them up, He requires every one of His children to search the scriptures for himself. He does not want us to know His acts alone. He wants us to have an insight into His mind, purposes and plans. The children of Israel knew the acts of God, but, Moses knew His ways (Psalm 103:7).

1 Corinthians 14:20 is an instructive verse.

"Brethren, be not children in understanding: howbeit in malice be ye children, but in understanding be men".

Some Christians unfortunately are children when it comes to understanding. They always require someone to tell them what God has said, instead of going through the scriptures themselves. This is not right. It is possible to be a man physically but only a child in other things. In malice God wants us to be children.

There is an innocence that children possess, which God wants His people to have. God doesn't want you to be perfected in the wrong things of life. Rather, He wants you to be perfected in the right things. He doesn't want you to become a professional in the wrong things. If you must become an expert at anything, it should be in things that are praise-worthy. Become an expert in understanding, in wisdom and in knowledge.

It is possible to have a good understanding of science, or politics. You could even be very successful at your job, or be a celebrated businessman. But in 1 Corinthians 14:20 God is

Spiritual Understanding

not talking about that kind of understanding. As a Christian you should have perfect understanding of all things. Here God is talking about spiritual understanding, which is greater than all the rest. It is far better in every way than any other. Not everybody has it, and it doesn't come by human intellect, but by the Spirit of God. That means, you can have someone who is an expert in some other things, but little better than a fool when it comes to spiritual things. And God does not want His children to be that way.

Paul also refers to this in his letter to the Colossians.

"For this cause we also, since the day we heard it, do not cease to pray for you, and to desire that ye might be filled with the knowledge of his will in all wisdom and spiritual understanding".

Colossians 1:9

God wants you to be filled with the knowledge of His will for you. He does not want you confused or uncertain about His desires for you. He wants you to know what He wants you to do, and what He wants you to believe on every issue of life.

Unfortunately, instead of studying the Word of God for themselves, some Christians will simply fold their arms and moan, *'We don't know the will of God, we don't know what God might do, we don't know what is on His mind. God works in mysterious ways, His wonders to perform.'* Have you ever heard that? It is a lie from the pit of hell designed to keep the child of God in ignorance. God does not work in mysterious ways. He gave us the Bible, and blessed us with the Holy Spirit, and declared that as many as are led by the Spirit of God they are the sons of God.**(Romans 8:14)** And in this scripture **(Colossians 1:9)**, Paul prays for this church that they might be filled with the knowledge of God's will. Paul was praying by the Spirit of God, and if God wanted them to be filled with the knowledge of His will, it is proof positive that He wasn't about to do anything mysterious or unknown with them.

    To be mysterious means to be strange, beyond understanding, so nobody understands you. Our heavenly Father certainly isn't like that. Jesus Christ came to declare God to us, so we can have a perfect revelation of Him.

    "**God, who at sundry times and in divers manners spake in time past unto the fathers by the prophets, hath in these last days spoken unto us by his Son, whom he hath appointed heir of all things, by whom also he made the worlds; Who being the brightness of his glory, and the express image of his person, and upholding all things by the word of his power, when he hath by himself purged our sins, sat down on the right hand of the Majesty on high**"

Hebrews 1:1-3

    This means that by looking at the life of Jesus, you could have an understanding of the nature of the Father. You will not only know the will of God, but you will also find yourself

Spiritual Understanding

doing it when you follow Jesus. Jesus said to his disciples, *'I've told you everything about my Father.'* (John 15:15-16). He called them His friends, He told them, *"The servant doesn't know everything that the master does, but I have poured my heart to you"*. (John 15:13) Then he also told them,

I have yet many things to say unto you, but ye cannot bear them now. Howbeit when he, the Spirit of truth, is come, he will guide you into all truth: for he shall not speak of himself; but whatsoever he shall hear, that shall he speak: and he will show you things to come.

John 16: 12,13

So when in Colossians 1:9, Paul prayed for the church at Colosse, that they should be filled with the knowledge of God's will, in all wisdom and spiritual understanding, He was referring to spiritual things.

To understand spiritual things really refers to understanding the Word of God; understanding the things that are relevant to the kingdom of God. There are many things that we don't ask questions about, we just know them in our spirit. I was not there when Jesus rose from the dead but I believe it with all my heart. If you ask me, *'How do you know?'* I can only tell you I believe it. And if you are a Christian too, you know it this way, because you also were not there. You would have to be about 2,000 years of age to have been in Jerusalem when Jesus rose from the dead.

The Bible says the Spirit of God bears witness with our

The Oil and The Mantle

spirit that we are the children of God. If you ask me, *'Are you born again?*, I will answer that I know I am born-again . If you go on to ask me, *How do you know?*, I can only say I know it in my spirit. The Holy Ghost bears witness with my spirit that I am a child of God. I know it deep down in me. So it is the same way with the resurrection of our Lord Jesus from the dead. I was not there, but I know it deep down in me. The Bible says so and I believe it.

I once asked a young guy a question like this and he gave a very beautiful answer. He said it was, "an inner feeling".

The more you understand the Word of God, the more spiritually enlightened you are.

Let's look at some other scriptures in connection with this.

"I will instruct thee and teach thee in the way which thou shalt go: I will guide thee with mine eye. Be ye not as the horse, or as the mule, which have no understanding: whose mouth must be held in with bit and bridle, lest they come near unto thee"

Psalm 32:8-9

"For as many as are led by the Spirit of God, they are the sons of God."

Romans 8:14

You are not supposed to do anything just because somebody said it, neither are you supposed to stick to something

Spiritual Understanding

when it has been proven to be scripturally unsound, just because you have believed it all your life.

When you find out something is wrong, you should throw it away. Sometimes it is amazing how God's own children allow themselves to be easily deceived. Note that I said, " allow themselves", because it doesn't have to be so. But thank God! You cannot deceive the real Christian for long. If he is desirous to follow Jesus, it is not possible to deceive him for long. He may be deceived for a while but he will sure find out very soon.

Jesus said, ' **when the spirit of truth is come, he shall guide you into all truth**", and that is what He is doing right now. This doesn't mean you should say *'Okay now, I don't want anybody to lead me, I can lead myself'*. No! There are many ways the Holy Ghost leads us, and what is going on right now, is the Holy Ghost leading you through His inspired words in this book.

When Jesus ascended on high, the Bible says,

" **...He led captivity captive, and gave gifts to men ...And he gave some, apostles; and some, prophets; and some, evangelists; and some, pastors and teachers; For the perfecting of the saints, for the work of the ministry, for the edifying of the body of Christ: Till we all come in the unity of the faith, and of the knowledge of the Son of God, unto a perfect man, unto the measure of the stature of the fullness of Christ: That we henceforth be no more children, tossed to and fro, and**

The Oil and The Mantle

carried about with every wind of doctrine, by the sleight of men, and cunning craftiness, whereby they lie in wait to deceive.

Ephesians 4:8, 11-14

It means the Holy Ghost establishes these offices. Therefore when someone stands in any of these offices to minister, it is the Holy Ghost ministering to the saints through him. So right now as I am teaching through this book, the Holy Ghost is using this medium to minister to you. This is the voice of the Spirit to you right now. And the beautiful thing is that God never contradicts Himself. What He has said in His Word stands. Any other thing that other people teach you must line up with the written Word of God. That is the sure way you can know it is inspired by the Holy Ghost, because God will never contradict what He has said in His Word.

CHAPTER ONE

Being Established In Righteousness

" I marvel that ye are so soon removed from him that called you into the grace of Christ unto another gospel: which is not another; but there be some that trouble you, and would pervert the gospel of Christ. But though we, or an angel from heaven, preach any other gospel unto you than that which we have preached unto you, let him be accursed. As we said before, so say I now again, If any man preach any other gospel unto you than that ye have received let him be accursed.

Galatians 1:6-9

Through Paul, the Holy Ghost told the Christians at Galatia, *'I marvel that ye are soon removed from him that called you into the grace of Christ unto another gospel which is not another but there be some that trouble you and would pervert the gospel of Christ'.*

This is the problem many believers have today. There are some that would pervert the gospel. It really doesn't matter if there are thousands, and thousands of religions. They can not affect the gospel of Christ. Jesus said, *"I will build my Church and the gates of hell shall not prevail against it"* **(Matthew 16:18).** It just does not matter how many religions the world has, or how many religious leaders they have, or how many people attack the gospel to cast doubts on God's Word. They are not a problem to the Church. The problem is that many Christians come up with doctrines that are clearly not from the Bible. That is why Paul talked about some wanting to bring in another gospel, which was really not another gospel, but a perversion of the gospel of Christ.

It so important you know the pure, and the true gospel of Jesus Christ. You need to ask yourself which gospel you believe. It is equally important that you are established in Righteousness.

The brazen serpent of Moses

" And they journeyed from Mount Hor by the way of the Red Sea, to compass the land of Edom: and the soul of the people was much discouraged because of the way.

And the people spake against God, and against Moses, Wherefore have you brought us up out of Egypt to die in the wilderness? for there is no bread, neither is there any water; and our soul loatheth this light bread. And the Lord sent fiery serpents among the people and they bit the people; and much people of Israel died.

Being Established In Righteousness

Therefore the people came to Moses, and said, We have sinned, for we have spoken against the Lord, and against thee; Pray unto the Lord, that he take away the serpent from us. And Moses prayed for the people. And the Lord said unto Moses, Make thee a fiery serpent, and set it upon a pole: and it shall come to pass, that every one that is bitten, when he looketh upon it, shall live. And Moses made a serpent of brass, and put it upon a pole, and it came to pass, that if a serpent had bitten any man, when he beheld the serpent of brass, he lived. And the children of Israel set forward and pitched in Oboth.

Numbers 21:4-10

The people were bitten of serpents and God, in answer to Moses' prayer told him to make a fiery serpent of Brass and lift it up on a pole. Anyone who had been bitten of a serpent, and looked up at the serpent on the pole would live. And Moses did exactly what God asked him to do.

Now, I want you to observe this: there was no time in their history prior to this particular occasion, when God told them to make a brazen serpent; and after this particular time, there was no other time that God told the children of Israel to do it again. He never said it in their law, that whenever anyone was bitten of a serpent, he should make a brazen serpent and look upon it. So Moses did this for this time because this was what God said to be done to stop the plague, for the people had sinned against God. It was not God's instruction for healing anybody who was bitten of a serpent at any other time, it was done only for this particular case that we have read of.

I'd like you to observe something Jesus said in the book of John.

And as Moses lifted up the serpent in the wilderness, even so must the Son of man be lifted up: That whosoever believeth in him should not perish but have eternal life.

John 3:14 -15

We read in our text from the book of Numbers that everyone who was bitten of the serpent, when he looked upon the serpent of brass lived. Here, Jesus said that as Moses lifted up the serpent in the wilderness even so must the Son of man be lifted up (that means hanged).

Why was Jesus typified by the serpent of brass, which Moses made? In the Bible, brass symbolises judgement, and the serpent is a symbol of sin. **2 Corinthians 5:21** tells us that Jesus was made sin for us. When He was on that cross, He became sin. He did not become a sinner, the Bible says he was made sin. The serpent symbolised sin and brass symbolised judgement.

That means that sin was judged, and anybody who looked at that One who was made sin and judged should live. Jesus tells us that what happened in the wilderness was done because of Him, to typify what He was to come and do. This is to say that, on no account whatsoever should anybody try to lift up a serpent on a pole if he is bitten of a serpent. If you were ever bitten of a serpent, Jesus is now the answer.

The Bible also tells us that the sting of death is sin, referring to the serpent. That means that when sin tries to destroy us, the answer is Christ. That was the reason for the serpent in the wilderness.

But it is sad to note however that several years after the death of Moses, that brazen serpent was still hanging on that pole.

" Now it came to pass in the third year of Hoshea son of Elah King of Israel, that Hezekiah the son of Ahaz, king of Judah began to reign. Twenty and five years old was he when he began to reign; and he reigned twenty-and nine years in Jerusalem. His mother's name also was Abi, the daughter of Zachariah. And he did that which was right in the sight of the Lord, according to all that David his father did. He removed the high places, and brake the images, and cut down the groves, and brake in pieces the brazen serpent that Moses had made: for unto those days the children of Israel did burn incense to it: and he called it Nehushtan".

2 Kings 18:1-4

Several years after Moses died, Joshua led the people, into the land of promise. But where was the serpent of brass? Somebody obviously took care of it. Somebody kept it, and I trust that it was not Joshua. Moses left it behind and as the people journeyed, somebody picked it up.

The Oil and The Mantle

After Joshua, came the Judges of Israel, and somebody still had it and they began to worship it as well as testify about it saying, *'You know when I went to the farm, this serpent came out and bit me. I went back home and this brazen serpent of Moses healed my body'*, and when that fellow testified, another picked it up and then another got the news. 'Were you bitten of a serpent?' 'Oh yeah!' 'Then you should go find the brazen serpent of Moses'. And they went there and they found whoever he was that was in custody of the brazen serpent, and this fellow also looked up and was healed.

'Oh the serpent's got power, this brazen serpent's got power'. And so it was that through the days of all the judges, they kept the brazen serpent. God had told Moses to make the brazen serpent, but only for that time. The people had been bitten by serpents during a plague and God had said that whosoever was bitten by a serpent and looked upon it would be healed. It is possible that they had a lot of testimonies. The brazen serpent was healing a lot of people and that is why they kept it through the days of the judges.

Then came the first king of Israel, Saul, and they still had it; and after Saul, came David and they still had it; and after David came Solomon, and they still had it, and Rehoboam came after Solomon, and they still had it, and on and on until the days of Hezekiah, the king of Judah whom we read of in II Kings 18.

By now the brazen serpent had gained a lot of recognition. It must have gained some kind of honour from the people, because it healed a lot of people. It worked, and by now people were no longer waiting to be bitten of serpents before coming to the brazen serpent.

See, they figured if it could heal the body, then it ought also to have the power to bless their lives. They thought they could get anything out of the brazen serpent. And of course if it carried God's healing power, it ought also to have promotion power. So they went to the brazen serpent to try and touch it, and from touching they idolised it.

And they found themselves going on pilgrimages to the brazen serpent and from there they built a shrine so it could be preserved, and then they built a high place for it and worshipped it.

But Hezekiah, was a man of God, and when he became king in Israel, he destroyed the brazen serpent, and called it Nehushtan, meaning 'pieces of brass'. He was showing them that the serpent was merely an image made of pieces of brass. It was no god and they were wrong to idolise it. There was no divine power in it and he said, *'Since you're going to worship it, we are going to destroy it'*, and he destroyed it.

Some people would have said, *'How could Hezekiah dare desecrate the house or tabernacle of the brazen serpent of Moses the man of God? This brazen serpent that had healed so many who looked up to it. Now, he has broken it in pieces.'*

The Oil and The Mantle

But what did God say about Hezekiah ?

"He trusted in the Lord God of Israel; so that after him was none like him among the kings of Judah, nor any that were before him. For he clave to the Lord, and departed not from following Him, but kept His commandments which the Lord had commanded Moses. And the Lord was with him; and he prospered withersoever he went forth:"

2 Kings 18: 5- 7

This was a man of God, and he destroyed something that another man of God had used to perform miracles. Why? Because the people had turned their faith to it.

God did not want His people to build their lives around the brazen serpent, even though He was the One who used it to perform miracles in the wilderness. Whenever man turns his eyes to the physical thing which he can see or touch, he loses sight of God, and this is what happens to a lot of Christians. When God uses some material medium to perform a miracle, the people begin to go after that thing , instead of the One who has the power to perform the miracle, with or without that medium.

God may give a specific instruction concerning using a handkerchief to heal the sick, or anointing the sick with oil; that type of manifestation may be given for a time but, He does not want us to build a doctrine on that. Rather He wants us to live by faith.

Seeking after signs

An incident occurred during the time Jesus was ministering in Israel. He had fed the people and as they followed him, the multitude asked Him for a sign to show that He was from God.

" They said therefore unto Him, What sign showest thou then that we may see, and believe thee ? What dost thou work?

Our fathers did eat manna in the desert; as it is written, He gave them bread from heaven to eat.

Then Jesus said unto them, Verily, verily, I say unto you, Moses gave you not that bread from heaven, but my Father giveth you the true bread from heaven. For the bread of God is he which cometh down from heaven, and giveth life to the world.

Then said they unto him, Lord evermore give us this bread."

John 6:30-34

Jesus told them it was not Moses who gave them bread to eat but the Father, and that now, He has given them the True Bread from heaven which is He who comes from heaven and gives life to the world.

'Oh Oh', they said to him, *'Lord ever more give us this bread.'* What were they really talking about? Manna! You know they were not after what Jesus was saying to them. They wanted a sign; something to appeal to their senses; something they could eat. They did not desire reality, they were only out to satisfy their appetite.

" And Jesus said unto them: I am the bread of life: he that cometh to me shall never hunger; and he that believeth on me shall never thirst. But I said unto you, That ye also have seen me and believe not... The Jews then murmured at him, because he said, I am the bread which came down from heaven.
John 6:35,36,41

They didn't like that and they said, *'Is this not Jesus the son of Joseph whose father and mother we know. How is it then that he said I came down from heaven?'*

"I am the living bread, which came down from heaven, If any man eat of this bread, he shall live forever: and the bread that I will give is my flesh, which I will give for the life of the world. The Jews therefore strove amongst themselves saying: How can this Man give us his flesh to eat?"
John 6:51-52

The people were angry with Him because He did not give them manna to eat. They wanted a sign, but He said, *'It's my flesh, it's me.'* The manna their fathers ate in the desert was a type of the real living bread, it was a shadow of what God was going to do. Jesus is the real bread, and so there is no need

Being Established In Righteousness

for manna.

They did not have to look for manna, when the real living bread was there with them. Jesus is present with us today by His Word, and through the Holy Spirit, but God's children are being told that there is some other thing which can represent Christ to them; which can magically solve their problems in the twinkling of an eye, and so they find themselves going after symbols: the anointing oil, and the mantle.

This is not right! The use of such things should only be as and when specified by God. The children of Israel ate manna in the wilderness for many years, but when they entered the Promised Land, the manna stopped.

"And the manna ceased on the morrow after they had eaten of the old corn of the land; neither had the children of Israel manna anymore; but they did eat of the fruit of the land of Canaan that year."

Joshua 5:12

They didn't need manna in the Promised Land; you don't need manna in the Promised Land. You eat the real food. Moses told them prior to this time, that they should meditate on the Law of the Lord for it is their life.

Today, we are in the Promised Land.

"But ye are come unto Mount Zion, and unto the city of the livivng God, the heavenly Jerusalem, and to an innumerable company of angels,"

Hebrews 12:22

The Oil and The Mantle

We are living in the day when we can enjoy all that God has done for us in Christ. His work is finished and He is reigning through us. We don't need signs in the Promised Land. We have the reality. Jesus said, *"I am the way, the truth (reality), and the life." John 14:6*

The Truth of the Gospel

God wants to show you something and I think that it is important that you know this.

"O foolish Galatians, who hath bewitched you, that ye should not obey the truth, before whose eyes Jesus Christ hath been evidently set forth, crucified among you? This only would I learn of you, Received ye the Spirit by the works of the law, or by the hearing of faith? Are ye so foolish?, having began in the Spirit, are ye now made perfect by the flesh?"

Galatians 3:1-3

The flesh refers to the senses; what you feel, what you see, what you hear, what you taste and what you smell. Paul asked the Galatians, *'Are you going to live your life according to your senses now that you've began in the Spirit? How were you born again? How did you receive the Holy Spirit? These miracles that we do amongst you, we do them by the hearing of faith, not by the works of the law. How come you are so easily removed from the grace of Him who called you into a*

Being Established In Righteousness

perverted gospel? Paul experienced a peculiar kind of problem with the Galatian Christians. Through the influence of some Jewish Christians, they had come to believe that they should mix their faith with the law of Moses. They were told they had to become circumcised, and to observe Jewish festivals and traditions.

But Paul said to them, *"Behold, I Paul say unto you, that if ye be circumcised, Christ shall profit you nothing."* (Galatians 5:2) Faith in Jesus Christ alone is enough to live the Christian life, and we have no need of any other rituals to add to our faith. No need to supplement your faith with 'extras'. The work of Christ was finished on the cross, and there is nothing more to be added to it, so it's futile for a Christian to seek for other things to supplement his faith. You don't need things of the senses; what you can see, feel, or touch, to help you grow your faith. All these are unnecessary supplements, and for the most part evidence of your unbelief in the simple Word of God.

Paul observed this among the Galatians, and it caused him to write them a letter to address the issue. In that same letter, he mentioned an episode which I want you to note and learn from.

"And when James, Cephas, and John, who seemed to be pillars, perceived the grace that was given unto me, they gave to me and Barnabas the right hands of fellowship; that we should go unto the heathen, and they unto the circumcision. Only they would that we should remember the poor; the same which I also

was forward to do.

But when Peter was come to Antioch, I withstood him to face, because he was to be blamed. For before that certain came from James, he did eat with the Gentiles: but when they were come, he withdrew and separated himself, fearing them which were of the circumcision."

Galatians 2:9-12

Evidently, there were parties within the Church, for Paul talks of *'those who were of the circumcision'*, and they were pillars in the Church, James, being the chief. These men still believed in circumcision, as being necessary for salvation, and they tried to impose it on the Gentiles.

They had to have a great debate before they agreed that Paul and Barnabas should go and preach the gospel to the Gentiles, the uncircumcised (Acts 15), but they still distinguished between those who were circumcised and those who were not. You can see this attitude reflected in the actions of James the Apostle. Unlike some of the disciples who had followed Christ and heard a lot of the Word directly from him, James was quite deep in the law. You will discover from his epistle that he referred to the law several times in explaining certain issues.

When they met in the council in Jerusalem, and they were disputing about the circumcision. James agreed with Isaiah's prophecy that showed the Gentiles were free, but then he added that they should forbid meat offered to idols and abstain from strangled meat, and from blood. He found it difficult to take that there was nothing else required for salvation, but he had to obey because the Word said so. He couldn't go against it, but in his mind he still felt they shouldn't eat meat offered to idols.

That was why Peter was afraid. Actually, Peter had been at Antioch for a while and all this time he ate freely with the Gentiles, not thinking there was anything wrong with it. After all he went to the house of Cornelius, and the Holy Spirit came on Cornelius and his house, and filled all of them. So Peter didn't think there was any problem with that, and he interacted with them freely until some people came from Jerusalem, and fearing what James might say when he found out that he was mixing with uncircumcised folks, he withdrew.

But Paul saw it differently and rebuked him for it. At the council at Jerusalem, when the issue of food offered to idols was discussed, Paul agreed to it, but after a while, he said whether it was offered to idols or not was irrelevant because these idols have no power! *(1 Corinthians 8:4-6)*

James, and some of the others were 'of the circumcision'. This indicates that the type of background that people have often affect their message, and their preaching.

"For before certain came from James, he did eat with the Gentiles: but when they were come, he withdrew and separated himself fearing them which were of the circumcision and the other Jews dissembled likewise with him; in so much that

The Oil and The Mantle

Barnabas also was carried away with their dissimulation.

But when I saw that they walked not up-rightly <u>according to the truth of the gospel</u>, I said unto Peter before them all, If thou, being a Jew, livest after the manner of Gentiles and not as do the Jews, why compellest thou the Gentiles to live as do the Jews.

We who are Jews by nature, and not sinners of the Gentiles, knowing that a man is not justified by the works of the law, but by the faith of Jesus Christ, even we have believed in Jesus Christ, that we might be justified by the faith of Christ, and not by the works of the law: for by the works of the law shall no flesh be justified.

But if, while we seek to be justified by Christ, we ourselves also are found sinners, is therefore Christ the minister of sin? God forbid.

For if I build again the things which I destroyed, I make myself a transgressor. For I through the law am dead to the law that I might live unto God

Galatians 2:12-19

This is the point. **Our teaching ought to measure up to the truth of the gospel.** Any thing that puts men in bondage or fear is not the gospel. Paul said, *'If you want to preach the Law of Moses, go on, but count me out'*.

There is a true gospel, and it is a gospel that sets men free. It does not bind. Paul said,

"Stand fast therefore in the liberty wherewith Christ

hath made us free, and be not entangled again with the yoke of bondage."

Galatians 5:1

Anything which binds the child of God, and makes him a slave to the senses is not the true gospel. If you have to feel the oil on your forehead, or have a handkerchief laid on you to invoke what God has already given to you freely in Christ, you are in bondage to the senses.

You did not become born again, or receive the Holy Spirit through a bottle of oil, or a mantle. So you don't need them to live your life!

Don't allow yourself to believe another gospel. What Christ accomplished for you was complete. Faith, and not physical signs is what you require to live victoriously.

We walk by faith

Those men of the circumcision had been schooled in the law, and the law holds men in slavery to the senses. Paul said *'What I preach to you I got by revelation'*. John writing in 1st John 1:1 said, **"That which was from the beginning, which we have heard, which we have seen with our eyes, which we have looked upon, and our hands have handled, of the word of life."** John was still preaching from the senses here, *'Brother I touched Him, I felt Him, and so I know.'* Do you understand? That was his message. He was talking from experience.

The Oil and The Mantle

But Paul's testimony was different. He said, *'I was not there but I saw it in the spirit'* and that's better, because we walk by faith and not according to sensory perceptions. Thomas said, *'I'm not going to believe until I touch him, and I put my finger into that hole in his side and thrust my finger into the hole in his hands'*. Then Jesus appeared, and He said, *'Thomas come and touch me, put your fingers into this hole, put your hands into my side'*. At that point, Thomas cried out, *'My Lord and my God'*. But Jesus rebuked him and said, *'Thomas you believe because you've seen, but blessed are those who have not seen but have believed'*.

Peter in his epistle wrote concerning the Gentiles who believed on Jesus Christ even though they never saw Him. He said *' I marvel because you did not see him but you love him, you were not there when he walked the streets but you rejoice with joy unspeakable and full of glory'* **(1 Peter 1:8)** He marvelled at them. God has called us to the life of faith, to the walk of faith. He said in II Corinthians 5 verse 7, **"For we walk by faith and not by *sensory perception (sight)*.**

This brings me to today's backsliding; the issue of the anointing oil and the mantle.

CHAPTER TWO

There seems to be a lot being said about the great power of the anointing oil with a lot of controversy also accompanying it. What we need to do is first of all ask what it means to anoint or to be anointed. What is the origin of the anointing oil?

The Anointing Oil

To anoint means to rub, or smear so as to cause to shine. The use of oil for anointing has its origin in ancient times, and was used for various purposes. In the Pentateuch, God asked Moses to prepare a special ointment with which to anoint Aaron and his sons as priests. We also observe in 1 Samuel 15:1, 1 Kings 1:34, 1Kings 19:16 that the kings of Israel were anointed with oil for their office.

In these cases, it was symbolic of the Holy Spirit coming upon the man to empower him for his office. It was a necessary sign, both for the one anointed, and those he was to lead because they were a people who walked according to their senses. They could not see the Holy Spirit coming upon a man, but they could see the oil, and then they could say, 'This is God's anointed.'

Visitors or guests to a home were often times anointed

The Oil and The Mantle

with oil as a sign of good will and respect, and the sick or wounded were rubbed with oil as a remedy for their illness.

It was and still is an oriental custom, mentioned throughout the writings of the Old Testament Scriptures.

In the New Testament, anointing with oil is mentioned 5 times. Two of these involved Christ Himself being anointed with oil, first as a guest in a home **(Luke 7:46)**, and secondly symbolising His consecration as the Son of God **(Hebrews 1:9)**

The other three instances had to do with ministering to the sick.

The first case was in Mark 6:13. When the Lord Jesus sent His disciples out to minister to people and as they did, they anointed many that were sick with oil.

"And they cast out many devils, and anointed with oil many that were sick, and healed them."

Mark 6:13

Now the Bible does not say that Jesus gave them oil. Jesus never used oil to minister to anybody.

As we have seen, it was a Jewish practice, a familiar custom of their day. Actually it was done all over the East, among the Arabs and Orientals. They were used to the use of the oil in anointing people. They were familiar with it. It wasn't Jesus who gave them oil, for we never read that he went about carrying bottles of oil. No sir! He never gave them oil. If He had given them oil, He would have said something about it.

The Anointing Oil

They anointed many with oil because it was their custom.

Jesus in **Luke 10:30-37,** told us a story about a man who was wounded by thieves and he fell down. A priest came by and did not do anything about it; a Levite came and would not do anything about it, until a Samaritan came by. Samaritans are also descendants of Jacob, but they were estranged form the Jews. This Samaritan, the Bible says carried the man that had been wounded and rubbed his body with wine and oil. That was their custom in dealing with the sick, and actually they didn't just put a drop of oil on the forehead, they rubbed the entire body with that oil.

The last time anointing with oil is mentioned in the New Testament is in the epistle of James. You must understand that James' background affected him. His letter is addressed to the Jews in verse 1 Chapter 1 of the book of James. He says, *'James to the twelve tribes scattered abroad'* He's writing to his folks and they know about this oil.

"Is any sick among you? let him call for the elders of the church, let them pray over him, anointing him with oil in the name of the Lord: And the prayer of faith shall save the sick, and the Lord shall raise him up; and if he have committed sins, they shall be forgiven him."

James 5:14-15

This is one of the major Scriptures used by those who teach the use of anointing with oil as a panacea for all woes. This is where they got the teaching, but I want to show you that it is possible to abuse it.

The Bible says,

"All Scripture is given by inspiration of God, and is profitable for doctrine, for reproof, for correction, for instruction in righteousness: That the man of God may be perfect, thoroughly furnished unto all good works."

2 Timothy 3:16

So we can see that every writing of the Scripture is inspired by God. But notice what Peter said,

'Knowing this first, that no prophecy of the Scripture is of any private intepretation, for the prophecy came not in old time by the will of man: but holy men of God spake as they were moved by the Holy Ghost.'

2 Peter 1:20-21

This means that God gave the inspiration for the Holy Scriptures, but they were written through men, as they were moved by the Holy Ghost. Because of that human factor, sometimes you can find that the mind, or background of a writer colours his communication of the thoughts inspired in his heart by the Spirit.

For example, Paul was a learned man, a Pharisee before his conversion, and his letters reflect a high level of understanding, ands excellent communicative skills. Peter was an unschooled fisherman, and you can observe from his letters that his language is different from Paul's. Likewise, James' background in Jewish custom shows up in his communication.

Also you must understand that revelation is progressive. The book of James was actually the first epistle to be written, and so you can see that his revelation of the work of Christ was not yet as clearly defined as one would find in the writings of Paul. For example, James is the only New Testament writer to address the believer as a sinner. In fact he says, *'Cleanse your hands, ye sinners; and purify your hearts ye double minded'* **(James 4:8).**

From our studies in the previous chapter, we can see that he still held to Jewish doctrines, teaching, and practices, and anointing with oil was one of them. When you study the book of James, you're going to notice something. He refers to the law, saying, *"Brethren don't you know if you fail in one part of the law, you have committed sin in the rest of them, because the one God who says, 'Thou shall not steal', is the same God who says, Thou shall not commit adultery'.* He brings in the law and says; *'You ought to live as those who shall be judged by the law of liberty* **(James 4:11).**

Sometimes its difficult to say if he is advocating life by the law or be the new testament. He said, *'If you judge your brother, if you speak evil of your brother, you are judging the law. Don't you judge the law.'*

The Oil and The Mantle

But, brother, that law was judged according to Paul. He said the handwriting of ordinances that was against us was nailed to the cross. Study with revelation and let the Holy Ghost teach you. Even with all the accompanying testimonies it is easy to see there is something wrong with it.

This is a perversion of the gospel of Christ, because it puts God's people in bondage to another god. It just does not matter how many testimonies come out of it; it is not founded on the true gospel. I read a book the other day and the author said that the anointing oil is the Holy Ghost in a bottle. It's not true; it's simply ridiculous. He said that the oil is not a symbol, that it is not figurative. He emphatically declared that the oil is the Holy Ghost in a bottle. I was shocked, *'Oh there's no evil force that can come against the oil'*, he said. *'If you have enemies, when they come face to face with the oil, something is going to happen'*. Somebody needed a job and had been rejected. According to the testimony, he anointed his application letter with oil and they accepted him.

I don't have any trouble with the oil. See, the Buddhists perform miracles, Hindus also perform miracles. Even some of the Muslim leaders perform miracles. The juju priests too! But that's not enough. How come they can perform the same miracles they perform without the oil? That just means it's not the oil.

People have done to the oil what the children of Israel did to the brazen serpent of Moses. God did not intend for them

The Anointing Oil

to use it every time they had a problem. It was His appointed means of healing and delivering them on a particular occasion. But they abused it and began to call on it for every problem.

First of all, understand that the use of oil was a Jewish custom, not a Christian custom. Some Bible commentaries in connection with James Chapter 5 verse 14 say that anointing with oil was a common practise among early Christians. That's not true, because there is no historical evidence to attest to that statement except the one reference in James 5:14. It was not a common practise among Christians, it was a Jewish practise.

There are sacraments handed to the Church by the Lord Jesus Christ Himself (*a sacrament is an outward and visible sign of an inward, spiritual grace)*, and these include the Holy Communion, Water Baptism, and laying on of hands; but He never spoke of anointing with oil.

Don't I have enough money to buy a bottle of oil? Why am I against it? I'm not just saying this because I can't get the oil, I can get enough oil for distribution.

But who anointed Moses with oil? Nobody! Who anointed Elijah with oil? Nobody! But they were both men of God. Saul of Tarsus, the great apostle: was he anointed with oil? No! When they wanted to send him forth in Acts 13, they laid hands on him. That's the way of faith.

The Bible says when they had prayed and fasted, they laid hands on him and sent him away. There was no oil there.

The Oil and The Mantle

When specified by the Holy Ghost there is nothing wrong with the use of oil. But you have to realize it is for the babyish minds, those who are not yet developed in the spirit; they are the ones for whom you are to use this sign. And I want to tell you that the Bible says, signs are not for the believer but for the unbeliever.

"Wherefore tongues are for a sign, not to them that believe, but to them that believe not…"

1 Corinthians 14:22

The Bible says signs should follow the believer. **"And these signs shall follow them that believe;…"**

Mark 16:17.

We are not the ones reaching out for signs; we are the ones reaching out **with** signs. We are not the ones who should be looking for oil and saying *'Praise God, I have a bottle of oil.'* We are the ones who should manifest signs to the unconverted, producing evidence that Christ is alive.

Following those ahead

You can take examples from ministers and that's good because, you see, the lambs don't know the voice of the Shepherd because they are too young. They listen to the bleating of the sheep. They follow the sheep; they don't know anything about the Shepherd. They just see the sheep run one way and they all (the lambs) go that way.

The Anointing Oil

But I say to you, it matters who you are following. If a man tells you something which is not in line with the Word of God, you have to reject it and forget it. Yes, God can say, *'Anoint him with oil, and he will be healed'*. Sure, it can work; but when it becomes a doctrine, when it becomes, *'This oil is so protective, I will take it home and it will work for me all year round'*, then something is wrong.

When someone gives you a bottle of oil, to take to your job and keep in your handbag or pocket, or in your car, something is wrong: you are getting another god. You are beginning to worship Baal. You may not believe it but that is just the truth.

It's just like that brazen serpent of Moses – it was given to be used at a specific point in time, but the people began to follow after it, making it an idol. Don't follow after the oil, follow Jesus. The oil is merely a symbol.

A lot of things are going to come into the Church in the last days to turn the eyes of the believers away from the Master, the Saviour who redeemed them and they are going to ask for a God that they can see. Just like the children of Israel did in spite of all the signs they had seen. They said to Aaron, *"We want a god we can see like other nations"*. Then, they got a golden calf that they could see.

Some say, *"I know it is God who will perform it, but at least he needs something to go through"*. That's wrong. He doesn't need something to go through, He already went through One He wanted to go through and the name of that

The Oil and The Mantle

One is JESUS. Halleluyah!

"He sent His Word, and healed them and delivered them from their destruction".

Psalm 107:20

And who is the Word? It's Jesus. The Bible declares,

"In the beginning was the Word, and the Word was with God, and the Word was God...And the Word was made flesh and dwelt among us and we beheld his glory, the glory as of the only begotten of the Father, full of grace and truth."

John 1:1,14

You have to learn to discern the deception of the devil easily. Satan is not going to try to deceive you through a Muslim, or by sending a Buddhist to you. No! Do you think he is going to send some unbeliever out there? No! That would not be a bona-fide temptation. A real temptation can only come when a real Christian who ought to believe the Word of God, who ought to know it, begins to lead you away from the truth. That is a bona-fide temptation; otherwise, it wouldn't be strong enough.

A lie is not merely the opposite of truth; it is the perversion of truth. It starts out the same way as the truth but somewhere along the line, it bends off; so deceitfully that you almost don't observe it. The only thing that distinguishes the truth from a lie is the Word of God. So you have to enrich yourself with the Word of God so you can be very discerning.

"For the word of God is quick and powerful, and

The Anointing Oil

sharper than any two-edged sword, piercing even to the dividing asunder of soul and spirit, and of joints and marrow and is a discerner of the thoughts and intents of the heart."

Hebrews 4:12

The Word shows the difference. It is the discerner of the thoughts and the intents of the heart. The Bible says, *"All things are open to him, unveiled to him with whom we have to do"*, That is *the Word of God*. He will show the difference between the truth and the lie.

The lie may sound so good, but it does not matter. It may be in office for a long time, but that does not turn it into the truth. No matter how many testimonies you receive on it, you can get more by speaking the word of God. *'I poured oil on my head, thank God the headache went.'* Don't pour oil! Watch that headache go as you speak the Word of God.

CHAPTER THREE

The Mantle

The mantle is another questionable method of ministry. I see a lot of Christians today holding their handkerchiefs and they say they have a mantle. I want to address the issue of the use of Handkerchiefs in the Church today. How right or how wrong is it? The best way to show that is to guide you through the scriptures so that you can trace the whole thing from its fundamental teachings up to the present day.

I don't know why so many Christians would rather hallow their handkerchiefs, I don't know why they believe it is of God and I dare say they are wrong. I would like to begin this study with the rod of Moses, so that you can learn from it.

A lot of ministers urge people to go for handkerchiefs and even at certain points in their messages instruct everyone to bring out their "mantles". Some even have two, for the 'double portion'. It's amazing. Anyone who goes into the handkerchief business now would certainly make a lot of profit from it. It's really sad.

Who really is a Christian? What is it to be a Christian? Most people don't understand who a Christian really is. For if they really did, they wouldn't believe or do some of the stupid things they do.

The Rod of Moses

God had spoken to Moses from the burning bush that wasn't consumed and had told Him, *'I'm sending you to Egypt to bring my people out of bondage'*, and the man was scared, and asked, *'How am I going to do it?'* And God said, *'I'll be with you. You tell the people that I sent you.'*

"And Moses answered and said, But, behold they will not believe me, nor hearken unto my voice: for they will say, The Lord hath not appeared unto thee. And the Lord said unto him, What is that in thine hand? And he said, A rod.

And he said, Cast it on the ground. And he cast it on the ground, and it became a serpent; and Moses fled from before it. And the Lord said unto Moses, Put forth thine hand and take it by the tail. And he put forth his hand, and caught it, and it became a rod, in his hand. And Moses said unto the Lord, O my Lord, I am not eloquent, neither heretofore, nor since thou hast spoken unto thy servant: but I am slow of speech, and of a slow tongue.

And the Lord said unto him, Who hath made man's mouth? or who maketh the dumb, or deaf, or the seeing, or the blind? have not I the Lord? Now therefore go, and I will be

The Mantle

with thy mouth, and teach thee what thou shalt say. And he said, O my Lord, send, I pray thee, by the hand of him whom thou wilt send. And the anger of the Lord was kindled against Moses, and He said, Is not Aaron the Levite thy brother? I know that he can speak well. And also, behold, he cometh forth to meet thee: and when he seeth thee, he will be glad in his heart. And thou shall speak unto him and put words in his mouth: and I will be thy mouth, and with his mouth, and will teach you what you shall do. And he shall be thy spokesman unto the people: and he shall be, even he shall be to thee instead of a mouth, and thou shalt be to him instead of God. And thou shalt take this rod in thy hand wherewith thou shalt do signs.

Exodus 4:1-4; 10-17

I want you to observe something God said in verse 17. He said, *'With this rod you shall do great signs. Take it with you.'* So Moses took the rod in his hands and began to work with it. This rod later became the rod of Aaron, Moses' spokesman.

"And the Lord spake unto Moses and unto Aaron, saying, When Pharaoh shall speak unto you, saying, Shew a miracle for you: then thou shalt say unto Aaron, Take thy rod, and cast it before Pharaoh, and it shall become a serpent.

Exodus 7:8-9

Apparently, Moses and Aaron were together in this ministry, because God told Moses, " *You shall be to him in-*

The Oil and The Mantle

stead of God and He instead of a mouth to you and Aaron shall be your prophet and you a God to Pharaoh.' Moses was as God to Aaron, and Aaron spoke and acted for him to Pharaoh, so when God said to him, *'Moses cast down your rod in front of Pharaoh'*, Moses standing in the place of God spoke to Aaron and said to him, *'Cast down your rod.'* That means that Moses' rod was in the custody of Aaron.

I want you to notice something here which is very important, God said, *'Take thy rod and cast it in front of Pharaoh and it shall become a serpent.'* Did you notice that it's that same rod that Moses tells Aaron to cast before Pharaoh? He didn't say, *'Cast my rod'*, he said, *'Cast thy rod'*

So here we see he is talking about the same rod with which he was to do signs. It was that same rod of Moses that was cast to the ground by Aaron that became a serpent and you remember the story in verse 10. The Bible says,

" **And Moses and Aaron went in unto Pharaoh, and they did so as the Lord had commanded: and Aaron cast down his rod before Pharaoh, and before his servants, and it became a serpent. Then Pharaoh also called the wise men and the sorcerers: now the magicians of Egypt, they also did in like manner with their enchantments. For they cast down every man his rod, and they became serpents: but Aaron's rod swallowed up their rods.** Exodus 7:10-12

The magicians and sorcerers of Pharaoh's court did the same thing; they cast down their rods, and they all turned to

The Mantle

serpents, but something beautiful happened which we read in verse 12. Aaron's rod swallowed up theirs. Glory to God!

Now later on, after the people had come out of Egypt, Aaron became the High Priest. He was God's representative to the people. But something happened to this rod that I would like to show you.

One day, the people became rebellious against God, and they grumbled against Moses and Aaron. And God said, *'I want to show you whom I have chosen from among you as priest'*. He said to Moses and Aaron, *'I want you to tell all of the twelve tribes of the children of Israel to come and present a rod before me; a rod for a tribe, and I will show which one I have chosen.'*

'And the Lord spake unto Moses, saying, Speak unto the children of Israel, and take of every one of them a rod according to the house of their fathers, of all their princes according to the house of their fathers twelve rods: Write thou every man's name upon his rod. And thou shalt write Aaron's name upon the rod of Levi: for one rod shall be for the head of the house of their fathers. And thou shalt lay them up in the tabernacle of the congregation before the testimony, where I will meet with you. And it shall come to pass, that the man's rod, whom I shall choose, shall blossom: And I will make to cease from me the murmurings of the children of Israel, whereby they murmur against you.

And Moses spake unto the children of Israel, and every

one of their princes gave him a rod apiece, for each prince one, according to their fathers' houses, even twelve rods: and the rod of Aaron was among their rods. And Moses laid up the rods before the Lord in the tabernacle of witness.

And it came to pass, that on the morrow, Moses went into the tabernacle of witness; and, behold, the rod of Aaron for the house of Levi was budded, and brought forth buds, and bloomed blossoms, and yielded almonds. And Moses brought out all the rods from before the Lord unto all the children of Israel: and they looked, and took every man his rod. And the Lord said unto Moses, Bring Aaron's rod again before the testimony, to be kept for a token against the rebels; and thou shalt quite take away their murmurings from me, that they die not.

And Moses did as the Lord commanded him, so did He."

Numbers 17:1-11

The Bible tells us that Aaron's rod budded. God breathed life into it, and it budded, and that showed the people that Aaron was chosen of God, and the tribe of Levi. Now, after this, the rod was taken into the presence of God. It was kept in the presence of God, and in the New Testament, the book of Hebrews testifies to this.

"And after the second veil, the tabernacle which is called the Holiest of all; which had the golden censer, and the ark of the covenant overlaid round about with gold, wherein was the golden pot that had manna and Aaron's rod that budded."

Hebrews 9:3-4a

That was where Aaron's rod that budded ended up being kept: in the ark of the testimony in the presence of the Lord. The point is this: I want you to observe something in the development of the use of the rod of Moses. We now can see where it was in the days of Moses. It was in the ark. Moses no longer carried about the rod. God said '... *bring it and keep it in the tabernacle of testimony. Keep it in there and use only when the Lord requires it to be used.*

Now sometime during the period of their history in Exodus Chapter 17, something happened to the children of Israel. They became thirsty for water, and murmured against Moses.

"**And all the congregation of the children of Israel journeyed from the wilderness of Sin, after their journeys, according to the commandment of the Lord, and pitched in Rephidim: and there was no water for the people to drink.**

Wherefore the people did chide with Moses, and said, Give us water that we may drink. And Moses said unto them, Why chide ye with me? Wherefore do ye tempt the Lord? And the people thirsted there for water; and the people murmured

The Oil and The Mantle

against Moses, and said, Wherefore is this that thou hast brought us up out of Egypt, to kill us and our children and our cattle with thirst? And Moses cried unto the Lord saying, What shall I do unto this people? they be almost ready to stone me.

And the Lord said unto Moses, Go on before the people, and take with thee of the elders of Israel; and thy rod, wherewith thou smotest the river, take in thine hand, and go. Behold, I will stand before thee there upon the rock in Horeb; and thou shalt smite the rock, and there shall come water out of it, that the people may drink. And Moses did so in the sight of the elders of Israel."

Exodus 17:1-6

God told Moses what to do, because the people were thirsty for water. They were so thirsty; they wanted to kill him. And he cried to God, and God said, *'All right, take the rod of God in your hands and I will stand upon the rock in Horeb and then you smite the rock, and water will come out of the rock and then the people can drink and their beasts also'*. And Moses did so before the elders of Israel.

But observe this closely, here in the 17th chapter of the book of Exodus, when the people got thirsty, the Lord said *'Take the rod and stand before me at Horeb, and* **strike** *the rock'*. Now, I want you to see actually what the New Testament says about that rock.

"Moreover, brethren, I would not that ye should be ig-

The Mantle

norant, how that all our fathers were under the cloud, and all passed through the sea; And were all baptized unto Moses in the cloud and in the sea; And did all eat the same spiritual meat; And did all drink the same spiritual drink: for they drank of that spiritual Rock that followed them: and that Rock was Christ."

1 Corinthians10:1-4

Spiritual meat refers to Manna. What it means in essence is that that manna that they ate in the wilderness spiritually typified something which was yet to come.

When they asked for water, God said *"Moses, I'm going to be standing on the rock in Horeb waiting for you, and when you get there, in the presence of the elders of Israel, I want you to strike the rock and water will come out and the people can drink.*

1 Corinthians 10, tells us that it was a spiritual thing. It was an allegorical teaching that God was giving to the people at the time. *"... For they drank of that Spiritual Rock that followed them: and that Rock was Christ."* (1 Corinthians10: 4b). When Moses struck that rock and water came out, it was a sign. It was foreshadowing something that was going to happen: that Christ was to be smitten for the world. Jesus said that **'Whosoever drinketh of this water shall thirst again: but whosoever drinketh of the water that I shall give him shall never thirst: But the water that I shall give him shall be in him a well of**

water springing up into eternal life. (John 4:13-14)

He was that Rock which followed them, for the Bible says, '... *and that Rock was Christ.*'

God said, '*Strike the Rock with the rod and water will come out.*" You see, as at this time the rod had not been taken to the presence of the Lord. Moses still held the rod. They had just come out of Egypt, and had just passed through the Red Sea. Now, follow carefully, because this is all leading somewhere.

Another time, the people got thirsty again, but by now the rod had been taken to the presence of God. Moses was not going around with the rod any more. God had said, '*Bring that rod and keep it in the tabernacle of testimony.*' It had blossomed in the presence of God. Life was now in it. It was in the presence of God. Moses, no more went around with it.

'Then came the children of Israel, even the whole congregation, into the desert of Zin in the first month: and the people abode in Kadesh; and Miriam died there, and was buried there. And there was no water for the congregation: and they gathered themselves together against Moses and Aaron.

And the people chide with Moses, and spake saying, Would God that we had died when our brethren died before the Lord! And why have ye brought up the congregation of the Lord into this wilderness, that we and our cattle should die there? And wherefore have ye made us to come up out of

The Mantle

Egypt, to bring us in unto this evil place? it is no place of seed, or of figs, or of vines, or of pomegranates; neither is there any water to drink. And Moses and Aaron went from the presence of the assembly unto the door of the tabernacle of the congregation, and they fell upon their faces: and the glory of the Lord appeared unto them

And the Lord spake unto Moses, saying, Take the rod, and gather thou the assembly together, thou, and Aaron thy brother, and <u>speak ye unto the rock</u> before their eyes; and it shall give forth his water, and thou shalt bring forth to them water out of the rock: so thou shalt give the congregation and their beasts drink. And Moses took the rod from before the Lord, as he commanded him.

And Moses and Aaron gathered the congregation together before the rock, and he said unto them, Hear now, ye rebels; must we fetch you water out of this rock? And Moses lifted up his hand, and with his rod, he smote the rock twice: and the water came out abundantly, and the congregation drank, and their beasts, also"

Numbers 20:1-11

You need to observe that this was a new instruction. The first time God said, *'I want you to take the rod in your hand and when you get there at Horeb, I want you to <u>strike the rock</u> and water will come out.'* But here, the Lord said, *'Take the rod and gather thou the assembly together, thou and Aaron*

The Oil and The Mantle

thy brother, and <u>speak ye</u> unto the rock before them.'

He did not say **"Strike the rock "**, he said, **"Speak ye to the rock"**. He was trying to teach His people His ways.

He said, *'Take the rod, gather the assembly and speak to the rock.'* And Moses took the rod from before the Lord as he commanded him.

You see, the rod was not always with him anymore, it was in the presence of the Lord. Don't get the idea that this man was moving around with this rod. No! The rod was now in the presence of God, but God did not want the people to think that Moses misplaced the rod. Remember it was kept as a testimony when they rebelled. God did not want them to think the rod had no power. He just wanted them to know the difference.

God was moving and they had to move with Him. God was moving, and He did not want to use the rod now. He was trying to say, *'I can bring water out of the rock with or without the rod'.*

You know, after the first time the rock brought forth water, the elders would have gone back, and told the story of the great miracle. *'We got to the place and Moses struck that rock with the rod and water came out'.* And the people were amazed. *'The rod of Moses, what a miracle-working rod!'* Well God said, *'I want to change things'* You ask, *'Why?'* It was because He had smitten the rock once and that rock was Christ. God wanted to change things, and He wanted to do it in the presence of the people, so He said, *'Gather the whole assembly'*. God was ready for a big showdown.

But you know, Moses got mad at the people in a way God was not mad at them.

Let's look at verse 10,

"And Moses and Aaron gathered the congregation together before the rock, and he said unto them, Hear now, ye rebels; must we fetch you water out of this rock?

And Moses lifted up his hand, and with his rod he smote the rock twice:"

Numbers 20:10-11

I can imagine that at this point, all the angels that were present there (because angels minister to God's people) were wondering at Moses with their mouths open, because they see that Moses was not about to talk to the rock. Moses took his rod and was about to strike it and they were wondering, *'Hey! He wants to blow it'*.

God said, *'Talk to the rock'*, but Moses turned the attention of the people back to the rod. But do you know what? It worked!

"And the water came out abundantly, and the congregation drank and their beasts, also"

Numbers 20": 11b.

The Oil and The Mantle

It worked. Somebody says," *Well, the oil worked, I prayed with the oil and it worked. Are you trying to tell me, it is not of God?"* Do you know what is in the mind of God about your oil? Do you know what is in the mind of God about your handkerchief? I can't imagine so many Christians going all over the place with bottles of oil and these mantles that they talk about. Something is wrong. It's about time we shouted them down.

Yes it worked, but let us look at God's response. The rod worked, the oil worked, the handkerchief worked. Somebody said they used handkerchief and it worked.

Supernatural things can also be worked by some religions of the world, but that does not mean they are of God. One time they told Jesus that He had a demon and that He was casting out devils by Beelzebub, the Prince of devils. And Jesus answered them saying, *'If I do cast out devil by Beelzebub, by whom do your sons cast them out?"* This means that their sons were casting out devils too. He said, *'By whom do they cast them out?'* He said those ones were using magical arts (all those occultic practises in casting out devils), they were practising exorcism. They were casting out devils, just as Jesus was also casting out devils. But there was a difference between Jesus and them.

Jesus said it. He said, *'If I by the finger of God cast out devils, then no doubt the kingdom of God is come unto you'.* What's the finger of God? That's the Word of God. The Bible says, **He sent His word and healed them, and delivered them from their destructions".** (Psalm 107:20)

That rock was Christ, and God said, *'Talk to the rock.'* but Moses went and struck the rock, yet water still came out of the rock. But here is God's response in Verse 12,

"And the Lord spake unto Moses and Aaron, Because ye believed me not, to sanctify me in the eyes of the children of Israel, therefore ye shall not bring this congregation into the land which I have given them. This is the water of Meribah; (Waters of Strife) because the children of Israel strove with the Lord, and He was sanctified in them."

Numbers 20:12,13.

For that act alone, Moses could not go into the Promised Land. God forbade him, and He died in the wilderness. God said, *'Because you failed to sanctify me before the children of Israel'*

The same thing happens today with those preachers who try to turn the eyes of God's people to the physical; to the oil they can feel, and the handkerchief they can touch; to these 'wonder-working' agents. They can never lead the people into their inheritance, just like Moses could not lead the people into the Promised Land.

Why was it so important? It was because that Rock was Christ, and Christ was only to be smitten once and after

His death, you don't kill him again to get life. You don't kill Him again to get anything that you want. Now, you ask and receive by faith. In the Promised Land, we live by faith. That's why **2 Corinthians 5:7** says, **"For we walk by faith, not by sight".**

The Mantle

Many people don't even know what a mantle really is. What is a mantle? A mantle is a coat, an overcoat; that is what the mantle is. It has nothing to do with a handkerchief. Though they are both made of some form of cloth, there is a great difference between an overcoat and a handkerchief. That little square piece of cloth is not a mantle. It could never be.

There were several people in the Bible who used mantles and they didn't use it for miracles. They were not called 'miracle mantles'. There is no such thing as 'anointing mantle' in the Bible. Samuel had a mantle and he wore it just like every other man of his day. You say, *'It's because he was a prophet'*, but Job also had a mantle and he wasn't a prophet. **"Then Job arose, and rent his mantle, and shaved his head, and fell down upon the ground and worshipped."(Job 1:20)** Job's friends also had mantles, and they were not prophets. **"Now when Job's three friends heard of all this evil that was come upon him,**

The Mantle

they came every one from his own place;...And when they lifted up their eyes afar off, and knew him not, they lifted up their voice, and wept; and they rent every one his mantle,...." (Job 2:11-12) It was just a coat, an overcoat.

<u>*Elijah's Mantle*</u>

This teaching of an anointing mantle actually originates from the story of Elijah and Elisha in 1 Kings 19:16. The Bible tells us that God had told Elijah first about Elisha, and how He was going to call him into the ministry. God told Elijah to anoint Elisha as a prophet. And when Elijah saw Elisha, he took his cloak (his overcoat) and cast it on Elisha and said, *'Follow me'*.

Did he anoint him there? No! The anointing was not in the mantle. If it was, how come later on, Elisha still asked Elijah for the anointing? He told the man to follow him. Elijah was a prophet of God, and the leader of a group of prophets, and he called Elisha to come with him. That act was a sign, an evidence to all of his calling. It was not the anointing but the calling. It did not mean that the anointing was in Elijah's mantle.

Remember when Agabus came before the brethren and addressed Paul, and took Paul's girdle and bound himself with it and said, *"Thus saith the Lord, so shall the Jews at Jerusalem bind the man that owneth this girdle"* **(Acts 21:11)**. Maybe we

The Oil and The Mantle

should begin to make girdles for ourselves so we might prophesy. Throwing the mantle on Elisha was just a sign, so Elisha would follow Elijah.

Let us examine another significant portion of Scripture concerning Elijah's mantle.

"And Elijah took his mantle, and wrapped it together and smote the waters, and they were divided hither and thither, so that they two went over on dry ground"

2 Kings 2:8.

Now, did he have to make use of the mantle? Not necessarily. He was a miracle-working man. A lot of times, different articles were used to perform miracles. You can read the life of Elijah. He did not always use the mantle like a lot of people would have us believe now. But this time, when he smote the waters with the mantle, they went through on dry ground.

Reading in context, we find that on this particular day, God had told Elijah he was going to be taken away to heaven, and he (Elijah) took Elisha with him across the river. Remember God had told him he was to anoint Elisha as prophet in his place.

"And it came to pass, when they were gone over, that Elijah said unto Elisha, Ask what I shall do for thee, before I be taken away from thee.' And Elisha said " I pray thee, let the double portion of thy spirit be upon me."

2 Kings 2:9

The Mantle

Now, let no man be deceived when he is told, *"Come over, God has promised to give you a double portion."* That is wrong. Don't believe it. God never said so and I can show you through the scriptures. (You can get more information on this from our book, *The Anointing for Living*)

Elijah did something here: he said, *'Ask what I shall do for you before I be taken away from thee.'* And the man said, *'Let the double portion of thy spirit be upon me.'* By asking for the double portion, Elisha was asking for the right of the firstborn; the right of inheritance after Elijah was gone.

According to the Law (Deuteronomy 21:15-18), the first son, or heir apparent should be given a double portion which was actually two parts, that is twice as much as each of the other sons to distinguish him as the successor (Deuteronomy 21:16,17). That was what Elijah wanted; the right of the first born.

Notice he did not say, *'Give me a mantle.'* He didn't say anything about the mantle. The mantle issue had nothing to do with what Elisha asked for.

"And he said, 'Thou hast asked me a hard thing: <u>nevertheless, if thou see me when I am taken from thee, it shall be so unto thee;</u> but if not, it shall not be so. And it came to pass, as they still went on, and talked, that, behold, there appeared a chariot of fire, and horses of fire, and parted them both asunder; and Elijah went up by a whirlwind into heaven. And Elisha

The Oil and The Mantle

saw it, and he cried, My father, my father, the chariot of Israel, and the horsemen thereof. And he saw him no more: and he took hold of his own clothes, and rent them in two pieces.

He took up also the mantle of Elijah that fell from him, and went back, and stood by the bank of Jordan; And he took the mantle of Elijah that fell from him, and smote the waters, and said, Where is the Lord God of Elijah? And when he had also smitten the waters, they parted hither and thither: and Elisha went over."

2 Kings 2:10-14

Elijah did not say the anointing would come on Elisha if he got a hold of his mantle. He said that if he saw him go, it was his. The mantle was not the carrier of the anointing. Then why did Elisha pick it up.

Every time in the Bible, from Genesis up to the New Testament, when a man tears his clothes, it never denotes something happy. It denotes something sad, a mournful event. In the New Testament, you find the high priest tore his clothes because Jesus said He was the Son of God (Matthew 26: 63-65). Paul and Barnabas tore their clothes at Lystra and ran in among the people because they attempted to worship them as gods (Acts 14: 11-15).

So, Elisha only tore his clothes as a sign that his master had gone. Do you understand? So, everybody would have to ask 'what happened? Well, the other 50 prophets saw it. The Bible tells us they were there.

The Mantle

"And when the sons of the prophets which were to view at Jericho saw him, they said, The spirit of Elijah doth rest on Elisha. And they came to meet him and bowed themselves to the ground before him.

And, they said unto him, Behold now, there be with thy servants fifty strong men; let them go, we pray thee, and seek thy master, lest peradventure the Spirit of the Lord hath taken him up, and cast him upon some mountain, or into some valley."

2 Kings 2:15-16

They saw what happened, but they may not have known that the man went straight to heaven because they said, *'Let's go and find him'*. That was the difference. He got the anointing because he saw and understood.

Now, Elijah's mantle, his coat, not his handkerchief, was what dropped to the ground. And the simple reason it dropped is because he did not need it in heaven. He had a different one to wear in heaven. Hallelujah! He didn't drop it for Elisha to pick up. Otherwise, he would have told Elisha, *'If my mantle falls on you, you can have it'*? Of course it was going to fall. He would not need it in heaven. Flesh and blood cannot inherit the kingdom of God, neither the things that are worn on flesh and blood. Amen!

So, Elisha did not pick up the mantle because it carried Elijah's anointing. He picked it because he had torn his own

The Oil and The Mantle

clothes. He took up the mantle of Elijah that fell from him and went back and stood at the bank of the River Jordan. And he took the mantle of Elijah, and did exactly what he saw Elijah do, and he said, *"Where is the God of Elijah"*, and struck the Jordan and it parted. This caused the other prophets to say, *"Behold, the spirit of Elijah doth rest on Elisha"*. Why did they say so? Because they saw the miracle.

Now, after this incident, you never hear about the mantle again. Elisha never spoke about the mantle. Check the Scriptures. If the mantle was the carrier of the anointing, how come Elisha did not use it? He never ministered with a mantle. That's just proof for us that it was not God's purpose for him to carry Elijah's coat and use it to touch everybody. Some ministers may say,*'Don't worry, I'm going to lay my mantle on you and you will get a miracle'*. But they are lying and they know it. They are deceived and are deceiving others. Just because some of these folks who have been Christians for a long time are preaching these things does not make it right.

A lot of the Pharisees and the Sadducees, were physically older than Jesus, who was just 30, but they marvelled at His wisdom. At the age of 12, He talked to all of those old men about the Scriptures, and they didn't know how to respond. He asked them questions, they couldn't, answer and He gave them the answers.

The Word of God is not known by your age. It is not known by how long you've been in the ministry. I have been

The Mantle

born again for over 20 years of my life, and have preached the gospel for over 15 of those years, yet that does not qualify me to push junk down anyone's throat.

I tell people it is not so hard for me to buy handkerchiefs and oil and distribute. I am not afraid to get them. But the truth is this lie is from the pit of hell. It's not true. Those who are preachng this are deceived and they are deceiving others.

Why do they do it? It's because they have no message. They have nothing to teach the people. Any preacher who sleeps all night long, and does not have the discipline to sit down to study, of course, will only call for testimonies through out the service. They read one verse of scripture and talk the people into a mess.

You can only minister that way when the people are still babes. The Bible says,

'When the Lord shall build up Zion, he shall appear in his glory. He will regard the prayer of the destitute, and not despise their prayer. This shall be written for the generation to come: and the people which shall becreated shall praise the Lord".

Psalm 102:16-18

It shall be written for the last generation, the Lord is building up Zion and He is going to build up Zion by teaching them the Word of God.

If you are ignorant of the Word, then you go for the

The Oil and The Mantle

'hanky'. The Bible says many signs and wonders were done by the apostles. Check the book of Acts, you can study in chapter 5. They had so many miracles, that they brought the sick on crutches and they laid them on the streets so that at least 'the shadow of Peter would overshadow them as he passed by'.

Why don't they talk about shadows now? Because it doesn't bring in any money. You want the oil? You can go somewhere where they've got it. You can get it by giving a love offering. This is not right. It is making merchandise of the Church. The Church is in ignorance but who is to blame: the ignorant. Because, God said *"My people perish because they lack knowledge."* **(Hosea 4:6).**

The Handkerchief

Now, let's conclude this, and find out how the mantle, Elijah's 'anointing mantle', became a handkerchief.

"And God wrought special miracles by the hands of Paul: So that from his body were brought unto the sick handkerchiefs or aprons, and the diseases departed from them, and the evil spirits went out of them."   Acts 19:11

This is a case where you have special miracles according to the Word of God; and pieces of cloth (not just handkerchiefs, but aprons too), were taken from the body of Paul to the sick, and they were healed.

Obviously the sick were not present there, or at least Paul could not reach them physically to lay his hands on them, possibly because of the large crowd, so these pieces of cloth which became charged with the anointing of God from the body of this man of God were placed on the sick, and that anointing healed them.

Now, this Paul never told the people to bring hankies into the house of God. He never taught after this that every one who needed a miracle should go and get a hanky, and place it on his body, on his car or on his house. In fact, we never hear of any one else doing so. It was a special miracle and should not be taught as a doctrine.

I have ministered using handkerchiefs or some piece of clothing. I have had these things happen through me and I will yet do them as I am led of the Spirit of God. I have used the 'hanky'. I have used the oil but they can only be used at the time the Spirit of God leads you to. Never tell the people to take a bottle of oil and keep it to use whenever they have a problem. You can not put the Holy Ghost in a bottle. No! He is a person. He has come to live in us. He does not want to live in temples made with hands. The Bible says Solomon built God a house, but then it also says God dwelleth not in temples made by hands. That bottle is another temple made by hands, so don't you tell me that God is the oil in there. The Holy Ghost is not the oil in there. That oil is a type of the Holy Ghost, and is merely symbolic. **Why do you want the symbol when you have the real?**

Listen to all the epistles written by Paul. You never find

The Oil and The Mantle

him telling the brethren to send all the hankies to him.

I was ministering to some people one time, and they were so many. I laid my hands on somebody who was not even a minister, and prayed for him and told him to go on praying for the people, and he started laying hands on them and some mighty things began to happen. But you know, it happened until the service ended and then the rub-off was over.

See, when you use things like the 'hanky', and they work by the Spirit of God, they become like any ordinary cloth when the anointing lifts. It's a rub-off at that time of the unction.

CHAPTER FOUR

Walking By Faith

In preaching, many things are allowed that will not be allowed when you are teaching the Word. Preaching is announcement; it is a declaration. In teaching, you unveil principles, you unveil realities, you unveil truth and that is why as a minister, before you teach, you need to study properly. In preaching, you may say a lot of inspirational things that may not have scriptural support. They are inspirational because of the state of your mind, and those of your hearers.

Some things are allowed while you are still a child. Paul said in 1 Corinthians 13:11, *'When I was a child, I spake like a child, I understood as a child, I thought like a child'*, but, he said, *'when I became a man, I put away childish things'*. We need to tell some of those folks who are using the oil and the mantle to put away childish things. We should not allow them to stay there for too long. It is God's Word that works. It performs miracles. You may ask how come these materials perform miracles if they are not God? They can, because the power of God is actually transferable. But then, if you are not walking in the light of God, something is wrong and you could get into trouble. God's power is transferable. You can transfer the

The Oil and The Mantle

power of God into a material.

These things are done at specific times during ministrations, but they should never become a doctrine for God's people to live by. A man of God one time left a chair in church, which he had sat on. He said anyone who would sit on it would have all his problems solved. People started making pilgrimages to the Church. *'There is a chair up there'*, they said, *'I will go there and Oh God, I shall surely receive my miracle'*. They came queuing up for the chair.

Signs are for unbelievers. *'Yes'* you say. *'But the miracle happened and that's what I want.'* Do you want a miracle that comes from God or do you want a miracle that comes from ignorance and disobedience? By now you should realize that supernatural things can come from other sources apart from God. Paul said, *'I refuse to abuse my power in the Spirit'* (1 Corinthians 9:18). Don't you understand that you have power and you can abuse it? Moses abused the power of God. He struck the rock when God told him to speak to it.

So then, faith cometh by hearing and hearing by the Word of God.

Romans 10:17

You can develop your faith. When you are born again, you get faith, but that little faith must grow. Do you understand? It must grow. Faith comes like a seed. As you use that faith, more comes. *Faith comes by hearing and hearing by the Word of God.*

Faith grows as you learn the Word of God. Your faith is built as you learn the Word of God.

But before faith came, we were kept under the law, shut up unto the faith which should afterwards be revealed. Wherefore the law was our school master to bring us unto Christ, that we might be justified by faith".

Galatians 3:23- 24.

This is marvellous. I wish you'd understand what this Scripture is saying. He didn't say the law would teach us about Christ. He said the law was present until we should get to Christ. The law never led anybody to Jesus. It was only there till Christ should come. That is what it's talking about. You have to read it in another translation to get a better picture.

"**Wherefore the law was our schoolmaster to bring us unto Christ that we might be justified by faith but after that faith is come, we are no longer under a schoolmaster".**

Do you understand? When you begin to learn the faith of God, you put the oil behind you. You put the handkerchief behind you. You speak the Word of God and watch God perform miracles. Do you understand? No more hankies, no more oil, but the Word.